Published in Great Britain in MMXXI by
Book House, an imprint of
The Salariya Book Company Ltd
25 Marlborough Place, Brighton BN1 1UB
www.salariya.com

ISBN: 978-1-913337-82-7

© The Salariya Book Company Ltd MMXXI

All rights reserved. No part of this publication may be reproduced, stored in or introduced into a retrieval system or transmitted in any form, or by any means (electronic, mechanical, photocopying, recording or otherwise) without the written permission of the publisher. Any person who does any unauthorised act in relation to this publication may be liable to criminal prosecution and civil claims for damages.

1 3 5 7 9 8 6 4 2

A CIP catalogue record for this book is available
from the British Library.

Printed and bound in Malta.

This book is sold subject to the conditions that it shall not, by way of trade or otherwise, be lent, resold, hired out, or otherwise circulated without the publisher's prior consent in any form or binding or cover other than that in which it is published and without similar condition being imposed on the subsequent purchaser.

Author: Roger Canavan
Illustrator: Damian Zain
Editor: Nick Pierce

Visit
www.salariya.com
for our online catalogue and
free fun stuff.

🌍 ADVENTURES IN THE REAL WORLD
1922 DISCOVERING THE TOMB OF TUTANKHAMUN

WRITTEN BY
ROGER CANAVAN

ILLUSTRATED BY
DAMIAN ZAIN

BOOK HOUSE
a SALARIYA imprint

Tomb of Tutankhamun

ANNEX

ANTECHAMBER

CORRIDOR

COFFIN CHAMBER

ANCIENT EGYPT

VALLEY OF THE KINGS, EGYPT

TREASURY

• 1922 DISCOVERING THE TOMB OF TUTANKHAMUN •

INTRODUCTION

Workmen were clearing the main Exhibition Hall of the Egyptian Museum in Cairo. Some were sweeping the marble floor, others hard at work with hammers and saws as they placed display cases in the centre of the hall. High above them, a young woman balanced on a rafter as she unfurled a banner. She let go and it unrolled downward.

The banner hung directly over the display cases. The big letters across it read 'The Treasures of Tutankhamun'. Below it read 'Now you can discover them.'

• ADVENTURES IN THE REAL WORLD •

To the right of the cases, in a darkened side room, was a table with small signs beneath two shadowy shapes. A worker entered with a torch and read 'Mummified cat, buried with the Boy King' and 'Mummified snake, Fourteenth Dynasty'.

He sighed and returned to the busy hall, muttering 'Nothing interesting in there. Back to the interesting stuff!'

The mummified snake wriggled angrily. '"Nothing interesting!!?" What are we? Boring? Old-fashioned? Hey, you with the torch! Didn't you read the sign? This is the Egyptian Museum, and it's full of old stuff like us. Don't you get it? And besides — why have you moved us into this poky little room? We were the main attraction out there until you showed up.'

'Sobek, don't lose your temper or we'll be thrown out with the rubbish.' Mau, the cat mummy, tried to calm her cobra friend. 'After all, it's quieter here — with no humans overhearing us.'

'But we had a lovely spot until this morning. Right in the

• 1922 DISCOVERING THE TOMB OF TUTANKHAMUN •

middle of things out there. Teachers, parents, toddlers, kids — everyone got to see us and learn about ancient Egypt.'

'That's true, but don't forget that lots of visitors have paid good money to see this Tutankhamun exhibition. And the museum always needs more money to look after its other attractions, including us.'

'Tutankhamun. Ha! I don't think that the humans can pronounce his name properly. A lot of them keep saying "Tut, Tut" as if they were telling a child to be quiet. Mau, be serious. Is this whole Tutankhamun exhibition really worth all the fuss and bother?'

'Well, you're asking the right cat. You know, I spent about 3,000 years with Tutankhamun, buried in his tomb. It was full of the most marvellous objects: gold, amber, colourful jewels. All of that stuff is part of the exhibition.'

'You mean the tomb itself is empty?'

• ADVENTURES IN THE REAL WORLD •

'Yes, but everything in it has been looked after carefully. And most of it has been touring around the world, going to museums like this one. Look at the labels on all those boxes — "Tokyo", "Moscow", "Chicago", "Lima". I couldn't go because I'm too delicate. Plus I don't like flying.'

'OK, so Tutankhamun must be the Boy King that they talk about, right?'

'Yes, he became Pharaoh when he was only eight or nine years old and he died about nine years later. Like all pharaohs, he had a fancy funeral when he died, and he was buried with lots of things to help in the afterlife — including, ahem, his favourite cat.'

'And his favourite snake?' Sobek was getting interested.

'Maybe, but I think that snake mummies had gone out of fashion by the time Tutankhamun was buried.'

• 1922 DISCOVERING THE TOMB OF TUTANKHAMUN •

'Snake mummies never go out of fashion. We're timeless. Where were we? Oh, yes. A boy becomes Pharaoh and dies a few years later. But there were loads of pharaohs buried in tombs. What's so special about this one?'

'The tomb is special because no one was sure it even existed. Robbers called tomb raiders stole the gold and jewels from the famous tombs, but this tomb remained a secret. No one would have known about the Boy King or his tomb without the hard work of Howard Carter.'

'Howard Carter? Never heard of him. Who's he?'

ADVENTURES IN THE REAL WORLD

• 1922 DISCOVERING THE TOMB OF TUTANKHAMUN •

CHAPTER ONE
AN ARTISTIC CHILDHOOD

By late afternoon the team of workers had left the museum. The display cases, with their glass fronts, had been assembled. Waiting to fill them were the contents of crates marked 'Tokyo', 'New York', 'Sydney', 'Lima' and 'Mumbai'. Some had been emptied, with their priceless contents lined up on the floor. Other crates were still firmly sealed, after their latest international flight.

Mau and Sobek made their way into the quiet hall and examined the new arrivals. Moving up to a large vase and stretching in front of it, Mau began to speak.

• ADVENTURES IN THE REAL WORLD •

'Yes, you have Howard Carter to thank for this exhibition. He was the one who discovered Tutankhamun's tomb in 1922 and then carefully recorded all the contents.'

'Did he grow up here in Egypt, hearing tales of the pharaohs when he was young?'

'He certainly heard a lot about the pharaohs as a child, but he didn't grow up here. He was born far away in a place called England.'

'I've heard of England. It doesn't have any deserts, does it?'

Mau smiled. 'No, no deserts. In fact, it rains a lot there. And when Howard was young, it was famous for its fog. Especially London, where he was born in 1874. That's only about 150 years ago — nothing compared to what we're used to — but a lot has changed in that short time.

• 1922 DISCOVERING THE TOMB OF TUTANKHAMUN •

'London is still a huge city, but back then it was the largest city in the world. And it was the capital of a huge empire – the British Empire.'

A COUNTRY CHILDHOOD

Money was often tight in the Carter household, so Howard spent much of his childhood with aunts in rural Norfolk. Growing up away from a big city like London gave him a love for open spaces, although the open spaces where he would become famous (the Egyptian desert) were very different from green Norfolk. Country living also instilled a way of dealing with the world patiently, without the rush of city pressures, which is a good approach for an archaeologist.

• ADVENTURES IN THE REAL WORLD •

Sobek began to look interested. He liked conquerors and armies and empires. 'Was it as great as Pharaoh's Egypt?'

'Greater. With conquered lands stretching all over the world. But conditions in the capital, London, were difficult for many people there. The poor were crammed together, and everyone had to put up with poisonous fogs that sometimes covered the city like a blanket.'

'What's fog?' Sobek asked. He only knew the intense sunshine of the Egyptian desert.

'It's damp and nasty. But I only mentioned it because that's what young Howard Carter would have known as a child. Not a great place to grow up. Plus, Howard was the youngest of 11 children. His father Samuel was a well-known artist, but the family didn't have much money. And that's why Howard–'

'That's why Howard sailed to Egypt to raid some tombs!' Sobek was pleased with himself.

1922 DISCOVERING THE TOMB OF TUTANKHAMUN

'Not so fast, Sobek. First of all, I was talking about young Howard, when he was a child. And the grown-up Howard was too honest to go about raiding tombs. But let me tell you about his childhood — it's interesting.

LEARNING ABOUT EGYPT

Europeans knew very little about Egypt until French military commander Napoleon Bonaparte conquered it at the beginning of the 1800s. By the end of the 1800s, Egypt was controlled by the British. All through that century, wealthy European travellers returned with souvenirs of that ancient civilisation. Most people, though, had to rely on newspapers for reports of new discoveries. Young Howard Carter was lucky: he got to know people who had actually visited Egypt and were keen to describe its wonders.

• ADVENTURES IN THE REAL WORLD •

'Because the family was poor, with so many children, Howard was sent off to spend a lot of time with relatives who lived far from London. They lived in a market town called Swaffham about 161 kilometres (100 miles) from London. You can imagine what a change of scene it was for the little boy: leaving a crowded house in a crowded, smoky city and moving to the countryside.'

Sobek was obviously more interested in this talk of the countryside. 'And that's when he started seeing more snakes, right?'

'Uhm, maybe. But England doesn't have a lot of snakes. And certainly no cobras like you.'

Sobek looked disappointed, but then he perked up again. 'I get it. Howard Carter was able to borrow a spade from a local farmer and begin his career as a digger-upper!'

'Hmm. He might have done some digging, but only to

• 1922 DISCOVERING THE TOMB OF TUTANKHAMUN •

help his aunts with their gardening. Plus, the grown-up Howard Carter would never describe his job as a "digger-upper". He was an archaeologist: someone who carefully studies the past. Yes, there's digging involved, but the main thing is to examine what's been dug up without accidentally damaging it.'

'OK. I still don't see what all this has to do with Egypt; helping aunts plant potatoes or whatever he was doing.'

'He was also doing lots of other stuff. Like his father, Howard had a talent for drawing and painting. He would sketch trees and flowers, and also some of the farm animals. And when his father visited, Howard would join him on painting outings. Those took the father and son to wealthy people's houses. Samuel Carter, Howard's father, would paint portraits of the owners' racehorses and favourite pets.'

'Including snakes?' Sobek didn't have much hope that the answer was 'yes'.

• ADVENTURES IN THE REAL WORLD •

'I don't think so, but the Carters did paint some cats. The funny thing is, the English didn't seem to know anything about making mummies. So in those days the only way they could preserve the memory of their pets was to have them painted.'

'No snakes, no mummies, planting potatoes, fog. I still don't know where Egypt comes in.' Sobek was losing patience.

'It does. Howard began spending more time at Didlington Hall, which he first visited with his father to do some painting. The owners, Lord and Lady Amherst, both loved Egypt and showed Howard some treasures that they had brought back themselves.

'They also explained how ancient Egypt was largely unknown to the outside world until about 70 years earlier. That's when Europeans began to visit the ancient monuments like the Sphinx and Pyramids. Some of them began to study the monuments and tombs carefully, to learn more about Egypt in the time of the Pharaohs.'

DIDLINGTON HALL

One of Samuel Carter's clients, Lord Amherst, lived in Didlington Hall, a large house close to Swaffham. Howard would join his father on visits to Didlington Hall. It was full of paintings and antiques, but Howard was far more interested in the statues and vases – souvenirs of the Lord's travels in Egypt. Amherst was delighted that the young boy showed such interest and he often invited Howard over – even when Samuel Carter was back in London.

• ADVENTURES IN THE REAL WORLD •

Sobek decided to try once more: 'And some of them might have dug in the desert sand to uncover more monuments and tombs?'

'Exactly! Archaeologists and others who were interested (called Egyptologists) would set up camps near where they expected to find ancient remains. And yes, because most of those remains were buried under the sand, they had to dig for them. In fact, they even called those camps "digs". Do you see where this is leading now?'

'Yes, finally we're talking about Egypt. And so was Howard Carter with his wealthy neighbours. Did they send him off to Egypt to do some digging?'

'Don't get ahead of yourself. Lord Amherst certainly enjoyed telling the young boy about our writing — hieroglyphics. You and I know how easy it is to read hieroglyphics, but Europeans couldn't, until they found a stone with the same message written in hieroglyphics and some later languages, including Greek.

'That stone, known as the Rosetta Stone, meant that archaeologists could read the messages on all of those ancient monuments and tombs. Amherst was pleased that Howard seemed so interested. And his wife, Lady Amherst, was also impressed with Howard's skill with the sketching pencil and paint brushes.

'They began to think that Howard might make a name for himself far from Swaffham.'

· ADVENTURES IN THE REAL WORLD ·

CHAPTER TWO
TESTING THE WATERS

Sobek wasn't stupid or silly, and he wanted to prove that to Mau: 'I get it — "far from Swaffham" means Egypt, so the story is finally beginning to make sense, thank goodness!'

Mau smiled. 'Yes, "far from Swaffham" certainly does mean Egypt. But you must be patient with those Europeans: they didn't realize that Egypt is the heart of the world, not some rainy little island in the middle of nowhere. England is far from Egypt — not the other way round.'

'Of course.' Sobek was proud to be part of an intelligent conversation, something he hadn't been able to have for about four thousand years. He was just getting warmed up: 'Plus, they keep calling our land Egypt. Don't they know that it's really called Kemet?'

'You're right. Kemet is the real name. It's far more poetic than Egypt. In their language Kemet translates to "the Black Land".'

'Yes, the Black Land. But I've always wondered how it got that name.'

'Just think of the mighty river that runs through the heart of our land: the Nile. And each year it swells up because of the rains thousands of miles south of us. The swollen river flows north, bringing rich dark soil with it and deposits it on the banks of the river. Some of that soil is so dark that it looks black.

• 1922 DISCOVERING THE TOMB OF TUTANKHAMUN •

'Remember that even now, most of our people live close to that life-giving river. And those archaeologists and Egyptologists concentrated their searches on places near the river as well.'

ANCIENT KINGDOMS

Ancient Egypt's history stretched over thousands of years, with periods of growth, warfare, hunger and military triumph featuring through that long period. Historians and archaeologists divide the history into many dynasties (linked to rule by a single family), but overall they view ancient Egypt as having three main Kingdoms. The Old Kingdom (2575-c. 2130 BC) is sometimes called the Age of the Pyramids, with the great pyramids and the Sphinx being built. The Middle Kingdom (c. 2030-1650 BC) saw Upper and Lower Egypt united under one ruler, with farming and irrigation developing. The New Kingdom (c. 1550-1070 BC) was the richest period of ancient Egypt, with the Pharaohs conquering more lands than ever. That was when Tutankhamun lived.

• ADVENTURES IN THE REAL WORLD •

Sobek was still in a clever, quick-witted mood. 'And that's where we now find Howard Carter, am I right?'

Mau smiled. 'You're right, or you will be right. He's not quite there yet. In fact he's still based in Swaffham.'

Sobek looked disappointed.

'But not for long,' Mau added. 'Remember, Lord and Lady Amherst were fond of their young artist friend, who was so interested in their stories of Egypt. And being so wealthy — and interested in Egypt — they had many connections in the world of Egyptology.

'They learned that a famous Egyptologist called Percy Newberry was planning an expedition to Egypt. And he needed an artist to record what he expected to find.'

Sobek sat up, or as close to sitting up as a cobra can manage, especially a mummified cobra. 'Aha! Expedition

• 1922 DISCOVERING THE TOMB OF TUTANKHAMUN •

to Egypt. Famous Egyptologist. Needs an artist. The Didlington Hall folks know an artist who's interested in Egypt. And his name is… Howard Carter.'

'You're absolutely right. Newberry was impressed with the Amhersts' description of Howard Carter. They insisted that although he was still young — only seventeen years old — he was very mature. He would certainly throw himself into his work and he wouldn't cause trouble.

'Newberry agreed to take Howard along with him. But first, he wanted the young artist to become even more familiar with the sort of objects that he'd be drawing and painting. He sent Howard to spend three months at the British Museum, which was building an enormous collection of objects brought back from Egypt.'

'You mean stolen from Egypt,' Sobek interrupted.

• ADVENTURES IN THE REAL WORLD •

WHO'S IN CHARGE?

Several countries competed to rule Egypt in the nineteenth century. Egypt had been part of the Ottoman Empire (based in modern Turkey) since the 1500s, but Napoleon Bonaparte of France briefly gained control around 1800. The Ottomans soon overthrew French rule but were not powerful enough to hold the country together. In 1882, the British defeated anti-Ottoman rebels. The Ottomans held on to power in name only, with the British remaining in Egypt and controlling most levels of government. This arrangement made it easier for foreign archaeologists (especially British ones) to get permission to set up their digs.

'That's an argument for another day, Sobek. Remember that most of these things had been buried by desert sand for thousands and thousands of years. The Egyptologists argued — and still argue — that their work actually helps the world understand our great land.'

• 1922 DISCOVERING THE TOMB OF TUTANKHAMUN •

'So when did Howard Carter begin to understand our great land?' Sobek was looking at some of the Tutankhamun treasure as he spoke. Mau could see that he was getting impatient to learn more.

'Yes, when Howard Carter finished that time in the British Museum he travelled to Egypt with Percy Newberry. It was 1891. They travelled up the Nile to two sites that Newberry oversaw: Beni Hasan and El-Bersheh. Both of those were cemeteries where senior government officials, called nomarchs, were buried.'

Sobek laughed. 'Of course I know what nomarchs were — my uncle bit one on the leg and the nomarch died. He was buried in a rock tomb with lots of possessions. Not quite on the same scale as this stuff,' Sobek was slithering through some of Tutankhamun's jewels, 'but pretty expensive.'

'Hmmm. Maybe he was buried in either Beni Hasan or El-Bersheh. And maybe — just maybe — Howard Carter came

• ADVENTURES IN THE REAL WORLD •

across that tomb when he had just arrived in Egypt. At any rate, Newberry put him to work right from the start. Carter was hired to be a tracer: someone who traces the wall images on paper that's almost transparent.

'He was good at tracing but would also use his sketch pad to draw or paint some of the other tomb features, once he'd finished the tracing, of course.

• 1922 DISCOVERING THE TOMB OF TUTANKHAMUN •

'You can imagine the pressure that he must have felt, having to get his tracings or drawings done before his lamp ran out of fuel. Light would stream into the tombs through the open door, but as you know, the Sun sets very quickly here in Egypt. More than once, Carter got caught out. He'd blown out his lamp because the fumes were getting too much for him and would count on the sunlight streaming in to light his way. Then, when the Sun set, everything would go pitch black very quickly. If he wasn't sure exactly where the door was, then he'd spend ages trying to get out.'

• ADVENTURES IN THE REAL WORLD •

'Ooh, that sounds tempting. Like all cobras, I can see really well in the dark. If I'd been there I'd slide carefully along the tomb floor, making sure that Carter didn't hear me. I'd get closer and closer, rise up with my neck flared out, open my mouth to get my fangs ready, and...'

'If you did that, there'd be no more Howard Carter, and no one would have discovered Tutankhamun's tomb, which means that you'd never meet me because I'd still be buried under all that sand. You wouldn't want that, would you?'

• 1922 DISCOVERING THE TOMB OF TUTANKHAMUN •

Mau seemed a little annoyed, so Sobek decided to get back to the story. 'Hmm. Howard Carter got lots of training as he painted or traced those tomb walls, when he wasn't lost inside the tombs.'

'That's right. But there aren't too many Egyptologists around, and most of them know each other. Percy Newberry introduced Howard Carter to the man who was the most famous Egyptologist of them all: William Matthew Flinders Petrie.'

• ADVENTURES IN THE REAL WORLD •

'Aha! Four names! He must have been important.'

'He was. And he was so good at his work that he wound up being knighted and called Sir William Matthew Flinders Petrie. But most people referred to him simply as Flinders Petrie. He was one of the most patient, careful people you could meet. He'd go through everything — and I mean everything — that was found on a dig and note exactly where he found it, what was with it, how many more items like it had been located, and what condition it was in.

'Flinders Petrie was also a good judge of people. He could tell that Howard Carter, although very young, was also very careful to preserve everything he came across — plus, of course, he had the natural artistic talent to record all the images. So the established Egyptologist then took Howard under his wing and invited him to work on the special site of Tell el-Armana. Howard had heard about that place, and knew that it was an ancient city built by one of our most famous pharaohs, Akhenaten.'

• 1922 DISCOVERING THE TOMB OF TUTANKHAMUN •

Sobek was impressed. 'A teenager investigating the site of Akhenaten. And Tell el-Armana wasn't just any ancient city. It was Akhenaten's capital!'

PETRIE'S ADVANCES

Sir William Matthew Flinders Petrie (1853-1942) was the most important archaeologist working in Egypt in the nineteenth and early twentieth centuries. He helped make Egyptology an academic subject for study, and not just an activity for wealthy thrill-seekers. Flinders Petrie insisted that every object that was dug up – no matter how small – needed to be noted and recorded. Those careful methods, which are now common in the field of archaeology, were already in place by the time Howard Carter had a chance to meet Flinders Petrie. Carter's own careful methods in his own digs later on show the influence of the older archaeologist.

• ADVENTURES IN THE REAL WORLD •

CHAPTER THREE

MAKING A NAME

Mau looked very serious and turned to Sobek. 'Here's something I heard one of the humans saying the other day: "It's not what you know that's important, it's who you know." That ties in with the way Howard Carter's career moved. He was certainly capable and good at his job, but he also had the knack of impressing the right people at the right time.'

'You mean like the way his father got him to meet Lord and Lady Amherst, who introduced him to Percy Newberry? And

• ADVENTURES IN THE REAL WORLD •

he introduced Carter to Flinders Petrie. Have we run out of introductions, or does Carter keep on meeting new people?'

'Oh, he does meet new people but as usual it's because he has impressed those that he's already met. Flinders Petrie spoke highly of this young Englishman (still in his twenties, don't forget) to anyone he'd meet. Carter had shown that his artistic talent was top-notch, and that he was patient and thorough in every aspect of a dig. Those are real talents, and people who expect world-beating discoveries every day usually become disappointed and leave.

'Now remember that at that time, in the 1890s, government departments here were usually called "the Egyptian Ministry of" or "The Egyptian Department of...", but the people in charge were usually foreigners. So it was with the Department of Antiquities. Its director was a highly respected French Egyptologist, Gaston Maspero.'

Sobek was following Mau's explanation closely as he wound

• 1922 DISCOVERING THE TOMB OF TUTANKHAMUN •

himself around a statue of the god Isis. 'Let me guess: Flinders Petrie introduced Howard Carter to Gaston Maspero?'

'More or less. I'm sure that Maspero would have learned of Carter's good work otherwise. Anyway, it turned out that Maspero and Carter became close friends very quickly. In 1900, Carter got a big promotion, which was a sign that people recognized him as one of the leading archaeologists at work in Egypt.'

'Sounds to me that it was a sign that he was friends with Maspero,' Sobek added.

'I'm sure that played a part. Anyway, he was made Chief Inspector of Antiquities in Upper Egypt.'

'Upper Egypt. That's the bit at the top of a map — the northern bit, right?'

'No. Those Europeans made things confusing with their names

• ADVENTURES IN THE REAL WORLD •

for things. "Upper" in this sense means "further up the river" – the River Nile, that is.'

Sobek thought he understood, but he was a little unsure, so he hesitated a bit. 'You mean "upper" means "further south" – closer to the source of the Nile?'

'That's right. And it's along that stretch of river where most of the ancient temples, tombs and cities were built. Lower Egypt was the stretch of the Nile as it flows north into the Mediterranean Sea. Around 1900, Lower Egypt was the commercial heart of the country, with important cities like Cairo and Alexandria. But Upper Egypt was more important for Egyptologists.'

'So becoming Chief Inspector of Antiquities in Upper Egypt was more of an honour than being in charge of Lower Egypt.'

'You're right, Sobek. And you can see how Carter's character matched the bits of the job that didn't involve digs and

• 1922 DISCOVERING THE TOMB OF TUTANKHAMUN •

excavations. Remember, he was patient and took great care with all of his work. That meant that he would supply detailed reports and other information to the Department of Antiquities of Egypt. Plus he was responsible for checking all the digs in that vast area.'

Sobek had begun to lose interest in all this talk about the 'official' bits of Carter's work at that stage. In fact, he began to get sleepy and his head started to nod slowly up and down. On one of the down swings it hit the floor, causing Sobek to suddenly become wide awake. And to prove he was awake, he tried to recall what Mau had just said: 'Vast area... digs... Um, what were the digs in that vast area?'

'Oh, sorry Sobek. Did I wake you?'

Sobek ignored the teasing and continued as if he'd never drifted off. 'I'm serious. All this stuff about filling in forms and making sure "this is in order and that needs repairing" is all right, but it doesn't get us any nearer to real digs, does it? And

• ADVENTURES IN THE REAL WORLD •

at what point does the pharaoh Tutankhamun come on the scene, if I may ask?'

'Yes, back to those digs. Now that Carter had established himself and had a reputation of his own, he could visit and even join in on digs in that area. Some of the most important work was carried out by a rich American Egyptologist, Theodore M. Davis.

'Davis had the concession to dig in the famous Valley of the Kings. The concession was the official permission (from the Egyptian Antiquities Service) to conduct excavations in that area. Everyone knew the importance of the Valley, which was where so many pharaohs and other important and noble Egyptians had been buried...'

'Including Tutankhamun?' piped in Sobek.

'Yes, yes, but you're once more ahead of the game. By the time Carter arrived at the Valley, around 1902, Davis and

• 1922 DISCOVERING THE TOMB OF TUTANKHAMUN •

other archaeologists had begun to think that all the important tombs had already been discovered and excavated.

'Carter continued with Davis's digs in the Valley of the Kings. Like Davis, Flinders Petrie, Newberry and other Egyptologists, he knew about Tutankhamun and the Boy King's short reign. Most of the others believed that either Tutankhamun's tomb was somewhere else or that it had been raided and lost to history. Either way, it wouldn't be found in the Valley of the Kings.

'Carter thought differently. During the dig in the Valley, he unearthed some pottery and other small objects with Tutankhamun's name on them. He told Davis about these and suggested that they were on the trail of the Boy King's tomb after all. Davis was still convinced that Carter was wrong and that those pieces were just a coincidence.'

Sobek piped up, 'Carter was right, though, and Davis and the others were wrong. They must have been close to Tutankhamun's tomb while all that arguing was taking place.'

• ADVENTURES IN THE REAL WORLD •

THE VALLEY OF THE KINGS

The most famous necropolis (city of the dead) in Ancient Egypt lies a few miles west of the Nile, on the opposite bank to the city of Thebes (now known as Luxor). The site was chosen because it was hard to reach, which – officials believed – would protect tombs from robbers. For nearly 500 years, from the 1400s BC, the rock on the valley's hillsides was carved to provide tombs for pharaohs and nobles. By the time Howard Carter arrived there, most Egyptologists doubted whether any more tombs would be discovered. Carter thought differently.

'That's true. And despite having yet more "government work" to do, Carter kept supervising more digging. And in 1903 he had his first in-depth look at a royal burial spot. The tomb of Pharaoh Thutmose I had first been identified in 1799, but Carter was the first Egyptologist to clear the main passage of the tomb.

'It was exciting to examine what archaeologists agreed was

• 1922 DISCOVERING THE TOMB OF TUTANKHAMUN •

the first tomb to be built in the Valley of the Kings, but Carter noted that tomb raiders had got there first. Exactly when wasn't clear — maybe thousands of years earlier — but none of the treasures that accompanied the Pharaoh to the next world were there.

'Oh well,' sighed Sobek. 'With such a thorough approach, and sensing that Tutankhamun's tomb must be nearby, Carter was bound to find it.'

'That's true. Except disaster struck. Carter lost his job.'

'Lost his job?' Sobek was astounded. 'But he was so careful, so well respected...'

'Well, he wasn't dismissed. He resigned. It was down to his responsibilities in looking after all those sites. There was some trouble at the ancient site of Saqqara, when guards and workmen tried to get rid of some troublesome tourists. Carter supported his men, but the tourists created a lot of trouble

• ADVENTURES IN THE REAL WORLD •

with the Egyptian authorities and Howard Carter eventually resigned in protest.'

'So he went back to foggy England?' Sobek was sliding across the gold mask of Tutankhamun.

TOMB ROBBERS

Over the years archaeologists have excavated the tombs of ancient Egypt's royalty and wealthy to find... very little. It's not surprising, since those tombs had once been jammed full of jewels and precious ornaments. They would be very tempting for thieves. Howard Carter and his team were constantly on the lookout for tomb robbers, but many tombs had been raided and emptied thousands of years before. Ancient Egyptian court records from 1100 BC contain confessions by tomb raiders who had stolen from the tomb of Pharaoh Sobekemsaf II, who had died 460 years earlier. We don't know what happened to these thieves, but many tomb raiders were cruelly executed.

• 1922 DISCOVERING THE TOMB OF TUTANKHAMUN •

THE SAQQARA INCIDENT

Carter's career as a Chief Inspector – and nearly his career as an archaeologist – ended suddenly in 1905. A group of rowdy French tourists arrived at Saqqara, the cemetery for the ancient city of Memphis. They barged past some of the guards and damaged furniture in the site's office building. Carter was summoned, and he defended his men (the inspectors and guards) and sent the Frenchmen away. Soon there was a complaint to a French government official in Egypt, accusing the guards of violence. Carter defended his men against this charge, but resigned from his post as a point of honour. For more than a year he had to scrape out a living selling antiquities and guiding tourists.

'No. There was nothing for Carter back there. His life and work were here in Egypt. But with no job, he soon needed to scramble to get money to live. Carter, who had been one of the most important men in Egypt, had to earn money selling trinkets and taking tourists to some of the ancient sites.'

• ADVENTURES IN THE REAL WORLD •

'Maybe it was time for another introduction? It seemed to work up to now for Carter.'

'I sometimes think you're a mind-reader, Sobek. That's exactly what happened. For a couple of years Carter struggled to make ends meet. In his mind, he could still imagine Tutankhamun's tomb waiting for him out there in the Valley of the Kings, but he began to doubt whether he'd have more chances to look for it.

'Then, yes, there was an introduction. In 1907 Carter met a wealthy British aristocrat, Lord Carnarvon, who had just moved to Egypt to recover from injuries he received in a car accident. Carnarvon had visited Egypt many times before, and he was keen to learn more about the country's long history — especially its ancient history.'

'Hmm. I predict a breakthrough,' said Sobek.

'I think you might be right,' answered Mau.

• 1922 DISCOVERING THE TOMB OF TUTANKHAMUN •

LORD CARNARVON

Howard Carter is not the only person whose name is always linked to the Tutankhamun discovery. The other is that of the wealthy British aristocrat who paid for Carter's many years of excavating before the discovery. George Edward Stanhope Molyneux Herbert (1866-1923), the 5th Earl of Carnarvon, inherited a large fortune and became even richer when he married a member of the wealthy Rothschild family in 1895. Carnarvon and his wife spent most winters in Egypt, where they also developed an interest in archaeology. It was during one of those stays that they were introduced to Howard Carter, and a bond soon developed between them.

• ADVENTURES IN THE REAL WORLD •

CHAPTER FOUR
ANOTHER VOYAGE?

"**D**id you hear something?' Sobek had slithered out of the mask and was looking worried.

'Just you sliding along that priceless object,' laughed Mau. 'All the humans are gone. Are you worried that the tomb treasure is haunted? Maybe you heard the ghost of Tutankhamun?'

'You may laugh, but I did hear something. There it goes again, a sort of squeak.'

• ADVENTURES IN THE REAL WORLD •

Mau sat very still. Then, behind the mask and not far from Sobek they both heard two distinct squeaks and then a little scratching sound. Mau joined Sobek and they both looked very carefully behind the mask.

Neither could see anything until they heard another squeak coming from near the floor. They looked down and saw a small mummified animal, about the size of a kitten but with no tail, pinned to the floor. The heavy mask had been placed on one of the mummy's paws, so it couldn't move.

'Finally! I've been squeaking and squeaking for ages for someone to get me out and you two just won't shut up and listen. All I hear is dig, dig, dig and Egyptologists and introductions, and something about Tutu...Tuta...Tuna.'

'It's Tutankhamun, silly. That's what all the talk is about, and why this exhibition has been moving everyone else around. Until this morning we were based just where you're sitting — er, pinned. We're stars of the "Egyptian Animal Mummies"

• 1922 DISCOVERING THE TOMB OF TUTANKHAMUN •

collection. But we got moved because the museum wanted to put their Treasures of Tutankhamun displays in the main hall.

'That tells you who we are. We still don't know anything about you. We can see that you're also a mummy, but you don't look like any animal we've ever seen here in Egypt.'

'That's because I'm not from Egypt. I am from far from here, high up in the mountain range known as the Andes. My name is Kututu, which is the Quechua word for "guinea pig". And Quechua was the language spoken in the Inca empire. Like the Egyptians, the Incas made mummies of their best-loved animals.'

Sobek was trying to imagine life high up in the mountains. He asked: 'But how did you wind up here?'

'First, could you please unpin me? Thanks. I wasn't meant to be here at all. I was minding my own business in a museum in Lima, Peru, when a workman said, "Look, there's another

• ADVENTURES IN THE REAL WORLD •

mummy. Pack it up." Before you know it I was packed in a crate and put on a big plane for hours and hours. And when they unpacked the crates here in this museum, a clumsy person put this heavy mask on my paw and pinned me down. And it's all because of this Tut, Tut, Tutankhamun, whatever that is.'

Mau corrected Kututu. 'It's not "whatever", it's "whoever". I take it you don't know about who he was?'

'Or pharaohs? Or pyramids? Or the Sphinx?' Now it was Sobek's turn to ask a question.

'No. But I'd like to know. After all, it seems that I flew thousands of miles to see this exhibition!'

'Well to begin with, Tutankhamun lived about 3,000 years ago. He became the Pharaoh, or ruler, of Egypt when his father, the famous Pharaoh Akhenaten, died. His original name was Tutankhaten, with the "aten" bit honouring his

• 1922 DISCOVERING THE TOMB OF TUTANKHAMUN •

father's work. Akhenaten had many enemies because of the way he changed Egypt. That's probably why the young Pharaoh's name changed to Tutankhamun: Amun was the name of one of our gods.'

FAMOUS ANCESTORS

Tutankhamun was the descendant of two important pharaohs: Amenhotep III and Amenhotep IV (also known as Akhenaten), who ruled over sweeping changes in the kingdom. Akhenaten had turned Egypt away from its traditional worship of many gods. Instead, he ordered temples to honour a single god, Aten, which was linked to the Sun and represented by a bright disc. Many Egyptians hated these changes and demanded that the country return to its old ways. His name was scratched off many inscriptions and statues of Akhenaten were smashed. The young Tutankhamun would need to decide between old and new.

• ADVENTURES IN THE REAL WORLD •

The guinea pig seemed less interested in gods than in the idea of a young boy becoming ruler: 'The exhibition sign also talks about the "Boy King". Was that Tutankhamun?'

'Yes!', Mau and Sobek answered together. Mau continued, 'And he's called the Boy King because he was only nine years old — maybe even eight — when his father died and he became Pharaoh, or "king", as it says in the sign.'

'That's very young to rule a city,' Kututu answered.

'A city?! He ruled all of Egypt, which had a mighty empire,' Sobek said angrily.

Mau was a bit calmer. 'That's right. The Pharaoh ruled all of Egypt, which stretched along most of the Nile, the longest river in the world. Our gods gave us that mighty river and each year they made sure that the Nile dumped a fresh layer of soil on its banks. That soil made it easier for our farmers to grow many crops.'

• 1922 DISCOVERING THE TOMB OF TUTANKHAMUN •

Sobek added: 'The Pharaoh was in overall control of everything in the land, and not just how crops were grown and sold to the people. He had to make sure that good people helped him govern: priests to keep the gods happy, judges, teachers and most importantly, the vizier.'

'Who was that?' Kututu asked.

Mau drew a deep breath. She looked around, knowing that she had to be careful in what she said. 'The vizier was the most important person in the kingdom, after the pharaoh. His job was to advise the pharaoh and to make sure that the pharaoh's orders were carried out throughout the kingdom. If a new pharaoh was very young, like Tutankhamun, the vizier would really be in charge... until the pharaoh became old enough to rule for himself.'

Sobek was getting excited: 'Like Ay, vizier under Tutankhamun. Everyone knew he was the power behind the throne. He became pharaoh himself when Tutankhamun died so young, without a son to follow him. In fact, some people even said that Ay might have played a part in Tutankhamun's early death, so that he...'

'That's enough, Sobek. We shouldn't be talking like that. Who knows who might be listening? Besides, that was just a wild rumour.'

The visitor was very interested now. 'So Tutankhamun really did die young?'

Mau stretched and paused. She needed to steer the subject away from dangerous talk as much as possible: 'Yes, the Pharaoh was only about seventeen years old when he died. He had married his half-sister, Ankhesenamun, when he was only eleven years old, but their two daughters died as babies. When Tutankhamun died, preparations were made for a royal funeral although the Pharaoh had no son to succeed him.'

Sobek wanted to join in. Mau was happy to let him, as long

• 1922 DISCOVERING THE TOMB OF TUTANKHAMUN •

as he didn't start accusing Ay of killing the Boy King.

'Our royal weddings were very important occasions. Because the Pharaoh was our link to the gods, we needed to send him to the Next World in style. Luckily for Tutankhamun, that meant that the funeral began in the sacred city of Thebes, on the east bank of the Nile. His father had abandoned Thebes and our traditional gods.'

Kututu asked, 'So his tomb was in Thebes?'

Mau took over. 'No, it was on the other side of the Nile in the Valley of the Kings. That's where pharaohs had been buried for hundreds of years. The first step was to prepare his body to become a mummy. That took some time, and when the mummy was prepared a special barge carried his coffin across the river. A procession then formed on the western bank.

'Slowly it advanced towards Pharaoh's final resting place. The barge with the coffin rested on a large sledge, drawn by oxen.

• ADVENTURES IN THE REAL WORLD •

Bald-headed priests wearing robes led the way, saying prayers and burning incense, while two women mourners stretched out on the slowly moving barge. Other women, dressed in blue, walked alongside shrieking and singing mournful songs. If a new pharaoh had been crowned, he would join the procession along with rulers of the different Egyptian regions.

'When the barge reached the tomb, the coffin was stood upright. A priest would walk up to it with a sacred golden

• 1922 DISCOVERING THE TOMB OF TUTANKHAMUN •

tool that looked like a small curving sword. He would touch the coffin near Pharaoh's head several times. This was called the Opening of the Mouth ceremony. It was very important, because it meant that the Pharaoh would be able to speak, eat and drink when he entered the Next World.'

BEHIND IT'S THE PRIESTS, AND ONE OF THEM IS LOOKING RIGHT AT US.

• 1922 DISCOVERING THE TOMB OF TUTANKHAMUN •

Gods and the Afterlife

The ancient Egyptians believed in a great number of gods, who controlled natural events such as floods and sandstorms. The gods kept the world in harmony, ensuring for example that the Nile flooded each year and dumped rich soil on its banks. Gods appear in many statues and paintings, often in the form of animals such as jackals or hawks. The Egyptians believed that cats were living versions of some gods, who could protect the pharaoh and guard people's houses. After Egyptians died, their spirits lived on in the Next World, along with those gods. The pharaoh was a link between those gods and ordinary humans.

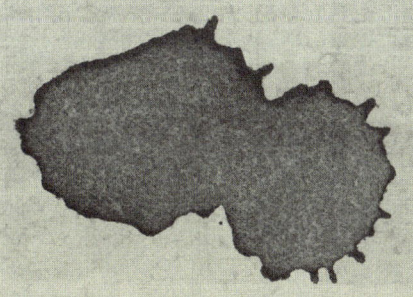

• ADVENTURES IN THE REAL WORLD •

A ROYAL TOMB

A royal tomb had to reflect the glory and importance of the pharaoh who had just died, providing him with a launch into the Next World. The tomb workers used hammers, chisels and basic drills to bore holes in the rock walls. Then plasterers, sculptors and painters decorated the chambers. The tomb would contain not just the mummified pharaoh, but offerings, ornaments and personal possessions to help the pharaoh in his Next World afterlife. Those treasures are what attracted tomb raiders from the earliest times. It was rare for archaeologists to find royal tombs still full of those treasures – which explains why the Tutankhamun discovery was so important.

Sobek didn't want to be left out of this explanation, so he added, 'After that the coffin was placed in the tomb along with precious objects and animal mummies, including cats.' He looked at Mau, who purred proudly, and then took over.

'When the ceremonies had ended and the pharaoh's coffin was

1922 DISCOVERING THE TOMB OF TUTANKHAMUN

placed in a stone sarcophagus inside a special chamber, the tomb was closed and the priests prepared a banquet outside it for the funeral guests.'

Kututu was fascinated. 'All of this is really interesting, but I have a simple question: why did Tutankhamun die so young? After all, there were many medicines and herbal cures, plus rich people are usually spared the diseases that affect the poor.'

EGYPTIAN MEDICINE

Medicine in Tutankhamun's time was a mixture of religion, magic and what we would call science. Egyptians believed that ma'at (harmony and balance) was central to life and that heka (magic) made this possible. For good measure, Heka was also the name of the Egyptian god of medicine. But records show that Egyptian healers were also skilled at setting broken bones and dealing with common ailments like headaches and upset stomachs. They mixed many natural ingredients – such as mint, incense, plant leaves and ground animal bones – to create pastes to treat patients.

• ADVENTURES IN THE REAL WORLD •

Mau considered this question. Sobek had already mentioned the rumours about Ay, so she tried to explain why people suspected the vizier. 'Well, it's true that there was a lot of bad feeling in Egypt around the time of Tutankhamun. Many people were still furious about the changes that Akhenaten had forced on them. And even though Tutankhamun had reversed most of those changes – reviving Thebes and changing his own name to refer to the old gods – some of those people were still not happy. But would they go so far as to kill a pharaoh, who they believed to be part-divine? I'm not so sure.

'Some of the humans who have been studying Tutankhamun recently have their own opinions about the Boy King's death. They rule out murder because Tutankhamun had a number of medical problems. He was buried with a walking stick, and he seemed to have some deformed leg bones. Plus he seemed to have had malaria and other serious illnesses. So it's more likely that the Boy King died of natural causes.'

• 1922 DISCOVERING THE TOMB OF TUTANKHAMUN •

WRITTEN OUT OF HISTORY

Much of the mystery surrounding Tutankhamun can be traced to his father, Pharaoh Akhenaten. By getting rid of the many gods that Egyptians had worshipped, Akhenaten cleared the way to worship the single Sun-god Aten. Later rulers turned against the measures of Akhenaten, so Tutankhamun (his son) was also wiped from most official records. That action might have helped to preserve the tomb and its treasures, since tomb robbers wouldn't have known about the treasures to be uncovered.

· ADVENTURES IN THE REAL WORLD ·

CHAPTER FIVE

BACK ON SITE

au and Sobek took turns explaining the rest of the story to their companion, who soon knew as much as Sobek about Howard Carter's efforts. Kututu was especially interested to learn more about Lord Carnarvon.

'I thought Lords and Ladies spent their whole time drinking tea in big houses in England?'

• ADVENTURES IN THE REAL WORLD •

Mau smiled: 'I think that Lord Carnarvon was tired of that formal life, with its afternoon teas and grand balls. He had a taste for excitement and the exotic. One of his passions was driving fast racing cars, but he had a bad accident in Germany which badly injured one of his legs. That meant that the excitement had to wait, but getting involved in the world of pyramids and pharaohs was certainly exotic.

'And that's what led him to seek out Howard Carter.'

Sobek wanted to show that he was also listening. 'But Carter didn't want to get involved with lords and ladies and balls, either. So why did he pal up with Carnarvon?'

'Well, a cruel person would say it was just for the money. But I think that Carter and Carnarvon really did become friends. Of course, knowing someone with lots of money – and willing to spend it to pay for your digs – must have been a real plus for Carter.'

• 1922 DISCOVERING THE TOMB OF TUTANKHAMUN •

Kututu agreed. 'Where I come from, high up in the Andes, the conditions are difficult for travellers. If you're trying to work as an archaeologist, with all the equipment, you also need to hire lots of local people. There's a lot of hard work to be done in those digs.'

Sobek didn't want to be left behind. 'The same is true here in Egypt: working conditions are tough and local people are the best to advise you on some of the most basic things. Like finding a regular water supply. Can you imagine spending months — even years — in the desert if you didn't know where the next jug of water was going to come from?'

'Or food,' added Mau. 'And although Carter had been working in Egypt for decades at that point, he knew what he didn't know, if you follow me.'

'I'm not sure that I do,' said Sobek.

• ADVENTURES IN THE REAL WORLD •

'Someone with less common sense or intelligence than Carter would have plunged right into excavations without making sure that he had a team of local workers that he could trust, and who could trust him. And you'll soon see how even the youngest members of that local team — people that "high and mighty" Egyptologists might ignore — can play an important part in the operation.

'Lord Carnarvon didn't speak Arabic and although he loved the idea of organising digs, he wasn't really very experienced. For those reasons, plus the fact that he had lost most movement in one of his legs, he saw that Carter would be the ideal partner.'

Sobek interrupted: 'Those are certainly good reasons to team up with Carter, but don't forget the most important reason. By the time he'd met Carnarvon, he'd already excavated six royal tombs. That's excellent experience, if you ask me.' And he looked over to Kututu as if to say 'Mau's not the only expert in this museum.'

• 1922 DISCOVERING THE TOMB OF TUTANKHAMUN •

And it was Mau who spoke next: 'Yes, I'm sure that Carnarvon recognised that skill. And the first excavations he asked Carter to organise were near the sacred city of Thebes. Carnarvon knew that some important nobles from ancient Egypt were buried there.

'The work moved ahead, with Carter managing to uncover some interesting — but not unbelievable — objects to shed more light on that period of Egyptian history. It must have been frustrating for Carter to think that far more interesting remains lay hidden beneath the sands on the other side of the Nile near him, in the Valley of the Kings.'

Sobek hadn't lost his voice: 'And he'd worked in the Valley of the Kings already, with that American archaeologist — Theodore... Theodore... Theodore...'

'Theodore M. Davis,' Kututu completed the name.

'Good, you've been listening,' said Mau. If you could have

seen behind her mummy bandages you'd have noticed that she was smiling. 'And it's Theodore M. Davis who entered Carter's life again, in 1914.

'By then Davis was tired of excavating in the Valley of the Kings. He'd been there for years, finding less and less that was interesting. He was convinced that the Valley had long since given up its treasures. Plus, he was old. 77 years old. So in 1914 he decided to pack it in and let Carnarvon take over the concession for the Valley.

THE VALUABLE CONCESSION

Carter convinced Lord Carnarvon that their real chance to achieve success (and glory) lay in getting the concession to dig in the Valley of the Kings. Theodore Davis, who had that concession, knew about Tutankhamun but was convinced that he had already uncovered what little evidence remained of the Boy King's tomb. He wrote 'I fear the Valley of the Tombs is now exhausted' and decided against renewing the concession in 1914. That gave Carter the chance to move in and explore just where he wanted in the Valley.

• 1922 DISCOVERING THE TOMB OF TUTANKHAMUN •

'This was excellent news for Carter, who had never lost hope in finding the Boy King's tomb in that Valley. But although Carnarvon and Carter had secured the concession, the big "Find Tutankhamun" operation stopped before it even started.'

'Because of the First World War?' asked Sobek.

'Yes, it began at almost the same time as the dig was meant to get under way. Egypt prepared to become a battleground — just as it had been many times in the previous three thousand years. British troops poured into Egypt, on their way to fight in Turkey or preparing to overthrow Ottoman power here. You see, the Ottomans had chosen to fight against the British in the war.'

Kututu looked confused. 'I'm puzzled. Did Howard Carter become a soldier?'

Mau smiled patiently. 'Don't worry. This period in Egyptian history really was confusing. No, Carter didn't become a

• ADVENTURES IN THE REAL WORLD •

soldier exactly, but he did help his country's war effort in his own way. Meanwhile, he did his best to keep any fighting away from the archaeological sites. Luckily, the Valley of the Kings was well to the south of all that military activity.'

WARTIME WORK

Gaining the concession to dig in the Valley of the Kings was exciting for Carter – but the timing couldn't have been worse. In the same year, 1914, the First World War began. All of Europe and much of the Middle East found themselves swept up in the turmoil. Carter wanted to help his country (Britain), but was too old to fight. But he did play an important part. By 1914 he had become fluent in Arabic, which is spoken throughout the Middle East. He put that skill to use to work for the British government as a courier and a translator.

• 1922 DISCOVERING THE TOMB OF TUTANKHAMUN •

Sobek wanted to add his voice again. 'So the war ended in 19... 19...'

Kututu finished the sentence: '1918.'

Sobek wasn't happy to have the newcomer explaining things, so he continued. '1918. I knew that. But by the end of 1917 the fighting had moved on from Egypt and it was safe to think about excavations again.'

'That's right,' Mau agreed. 'And that's when Carter set to work in his big search for Tutankhamun's tomb. He assembled a team and gave them instructions about the careful methods that he expected everyone to use. He wasn't going to rush things – he never did – and he expected everyone, from other archaeologists to cooks and water boys, to respect the site.

'So work began. By the end of 1918, with the war finally finished, Carter's excavation was well under way. Carnarvon had been happy to pay for the entire operation, but he rarely

• ADVENTURES IN THE REAL WORLD •

visited the site. He had been to the Valley of the Kings several times before, so he knew exactly where Carter was focusing his search. But Carnarvon was spending most of his time back in England.'

Sobek noted, 'Maybe that wasn't a bad thing for Carter. Even though he got on well with Carnarvon, he might have felt uncomfortable having him around the whole time.'

Kututu nodded. 'Yes, I can see that Carter was a patient archaeologist who didn't expect miracles the whole time. And although he seemed to be friends with Carnarvon, maybe he worried that the rich friend wouldn't be so patient.'

'I think you're right,' agreed Mau. 'The arrangement probably suited both men. Carnarvon knew he had the best man on the job out here in Egypt, and Carter had the freedom to look for ideal sites in the Valley of the Kings. He had a team of local people helping him, and as we know, you need Egyptians to help you explore ancient Egypt.

• 1922 DISCOVERING THE TOMB OF TUTANKHAMUN •

'For about a year, Carter guided his men from one part of the Valley to another. Carnarvon kept the money flowing, but there wasn't much news to report back to him. Carter worried a little that Carnarvon might be losing heart, figuring that the other Egyptologists were right.'

'And that there was nothing more to be found in the Valley of the Kings!' piped up Sobek.

'Nothing? Just sand. There seems to be a lot of it in your country,' teased Kututu.

Mau sighed. 'Well, that did seem to be about all that they could find — sand. And stones. And the remains of tents and camps where earlier digs had taken place in the Valley. In 1919 Carter decided to return to England for a visit. It was a chance to see his mother and friends back at home. But more importantly, it gave him a chance to see Lord Carnarvon again. Carnarvon invited Carter to his home, Highclere Castle, where the two discussed their progress... or lack of progress.'

• ADVENTURES IN THE REAL WORLD •

'Was Lord Carnarvon getting angry or impatient because nothing much had been found?' asked Kututu. 'Even rich people who live in castles don't like to waste money.'

Mau answered, 'That's true. And what's more, although Carnarvon was a lord, most of his wealth came from his wife's side of the family. When they had married, his wife's family paid off a number of Carnarvon's debts...'

CARTER AT WORK

Howard Carter had developed a patient, systematic approach to all of his digs. Before the first spade began digging he had the site mapped out in the form of a grid. It wasn't enough simply to say when an object was discovered and what he believed it was – part of a necklace, a broken vase, or the fragment of a statue. He needed to record exactly where the object was found within the excavation site. In that way, he could link how each part of the jigsaw puzzle connected with other pieces, helping him to focus on where missing parts might lie.

• 1922 DISCOVERING THE TOMB OF TUTANKHAMUN •

'So he didn't want people to think that he was throwing her money away in a wasteful hunt for a tomb that might not exist!' added Sobek.

'Exactly. Carter would have known all about that side of things, so he needed to be sure to keep Carnarvon's interest alive. He did that by going through Carnarvon's wide collection of Egyptian objects and preparing them for public display.

'Plus, don't forget that Carter was a careful person. You've heard humans say "Don't put all of your eggs in one basket", meaning take care to have other plans if one fails. While in England, Carter also developed some business arrangements with galleries and museums that were looking to build Egyptian collections.

'Eventually, in 1922, Lord Carnarvon said that he'd return to the Valley of the Kings to join Carter in the hunt for Tutankhamun. Carter set up the latest dig in January and Carnarvon joined him a month later. Remember that these

• ADVENTURES IN THE REAL WORLD •

digs last what's called a season: anything from two weeks to several months.

'In this case it went on for months, but by the end of the season – with our hot Egyptian summer beginning to take hold – nothing had been found. Time seemed to be running out for Carter, and it came as no surprise when Carnarvon said that enough was enough and that it was time to give up.'

ENOUGH IS ENOUGH?

Slogging away in the Egyptian sun with nothing much to show for it isn't much fun, and Howard Carter and his team had to cope with it for five long years. But it was Lord Carnarvon (more than 3,219 km / 2,000 miles away in England) who was the first to lose heart and decide that enough was enough. What had seemed so promising in 1917 now seemed a world away. Even from England, Carnarvon could picture the desert landscape, with its surface criss-crossed with evidence of earlier digs. It would take all of Carter's skill to appeal to Carnarvon's fading dream.

• 1922 DISCOVERING THE TOMB OF TUTANKHAMUN •

'But were they really close to Tutankhamun's tomb all that time? Surely they must have sensed that they were almost there!' Kututu was getting into the spirit of things.

'Well, Carter certainly believed that they were almost there. But who can blame Carnarvon for deciding that it was pointless to go on? After all, no one else in the world of archaeology believed that Carter would find anything. But Carter's enthusiasm was enough to convince Lord Carnarvon to fund one more season of digs, but no more. This time, in November 1922, it was final. It's hard to say whether he did that because he felt sorry for Carter or because he really believed that they'd find Tutankhamun's tomb.'

Sobek was looking nervous. 'So the pressure was really on for Carter to succeed in this one last go!'

Kututu added, 'Carter must have hoped he'd find a hero to come and rescue everything.'

• ADVENTURES IN THE REAL WORLD •

Mau nodded and smiled beneath her bandages: 'As luck would have it, he did have a hero — and an unexpected one at that!

'Carter started a new dig within days of the news of "one last season". On his map of the Valley of the Kings he'd marked where all the spoil heaps (dug-up rubble) from earlier excavations were located. He had a feeling that they might find something beneath a particular pile of stones and rubble on the slope below the tomb of Pharaoh Rameses VI, who had died after Tutankhamun.

'Within three days of beginning, on 4th November 1922, Carter's hero worked his magic. Perhaps Carter deserved his good fortune because of the way he respected and defended his local Egyptian workers. In this case it was the son of one of his local workers who came to Carter's rescue!

'Twelve-year-old Hussein Abdel-Rassoul was part of the site crew. He was the water boy — very important in our

• 1922 DISCOVERING THE TOMB OF TUTANKHAMUN •

climate — and he made tea for Carter and his father. On that day Hussein was returning to the camp with jars of water. He stopped to find some level ground where he could set the jars down and began levelling out the sand with his foot. With one of the "sweeps" of his foot he felt something hard beneath the sand.

'Hussein swept some more, revealing a long, level stone. His first thought was to tell Mr Carter.'

'So Hussein had found the tomb! After Carter spent all those years looking! And it was a local boy who did it!' cried Sobek.

'Carter certainly felt confident that it was his goal. But he had been disappointed so many times over the years that he would need to make sure. He got his men to dig and sweep away the sand and rubble. Soon enough they had dug away an entire staircase, revealing the top of a mysterious doorway.

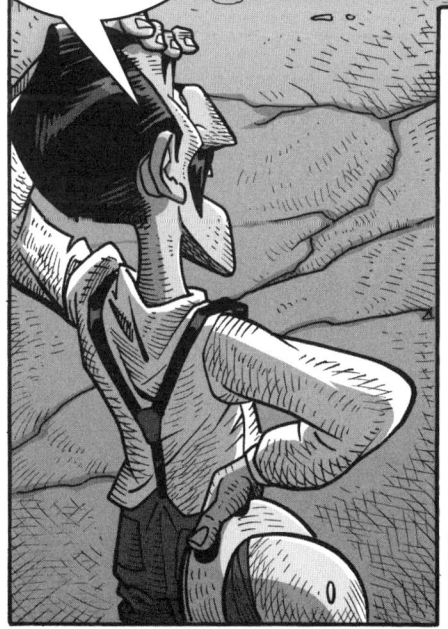

• ADVENTURES IN THE REAL WORLD •

'That was exciting enough, but Carter noticed something else immediately. The door was sealed with plaster, which still had royal seals intact — meaning that the door hadn't been opened yet.'

'The doorway to the tomb!' shouted Sobek and Kututu.

'That's certainly what Carter decided. And he was confident that he knew which pharaoh's royal tomb it was. But before he rushed in to open the door, he got his men to hide it again by filling the staircase in with sand.'

'Why?!' Sobek and Kututu seemed to be saying everything at the same time.

'Because Carter wanted Lord Carnarvon to share in what he felt sure would be a marvellous discovery when they did open the doors. He sent a telegram to Lord Carnarvon, reading "At last have made wonderful discovery in valley; a magnificent tomb with seals intact."

• 1922 DISCOVERING THE TOMB OF TUTANKHAMUN •

'Carter knew that Lord Carnarvon wouldn't waste any time in getting to the site. And he was right.'

· ADVENTURES IN THE REAL WORLD ·

• 1922 DISCOVERING THE TOMB OF TUTANKHAMUN •

CHAPTER SIX
TUTANKHAMUN'S TOMB!

'How long did Howard Carter have to hang around before Lord Carnarvon showed up on the scene again? The wait must have been terrible for him.' Sobek tried to make it seem like he felt badly for Carter but you could tell that he really just wanted the story to move on.

'Yes, and how did he travel that long distance?' asked Kututu.

• ADVENTURES IN THE REAL WORLD •

'Well, he travelled across Europe by train and then by ship to Egypt. Carnarvon arrived at the site on 23rd November 1922. His daughter, Lady Evelyn Herbert, was with him.

'Carter didn't waste time in returning to the new dig, this time with his wealthy sponsors as witnesses. He had the stairway cleared away for the second time. Being cautious, Carter also warned that what lay beyond the door still might not be Tutankhamun's tomb. All he could guarantee was that it had something to do with Egypt's royalty — the markings on the seals proved that — but it could still be just a storeroom.'

'That would be a disappointment, wouldn't it, especially after getting Carnarvon and his daughter to come all the way to Egypt,' Sobek said. 'You know, I think Carter must have known it was a tomb after all.'

Mau nodded. 'That sort of caution would have been typical of Carter, you're right. At any rate, they were soon going to learn the answer. With Carnarvon right behind him, Howard

• 1922 DISCOVERING THE TOMB OF TUTANKHAMUN •

Carter picked up a chisel that his grandmother had given him for his seventeenth birthday. He used it to create a small opening in the top left-hand corner of the door...'

'And then?' Sobek and Kututu cried out at the same time.

'And then Carter peered inside, using a candle to provide light.

'Carnarvon asked, "Can you see anything?"

'Carter's brief answer is famous: "Yes, wonderful things!"

'Howard Carter was right. The room was full of more than 700 magnificent objects. Some of them, such as small thrones and animal toys, were souvenirs of Tutankhamun's childhood. Three larger thrones are where the Pharaoh's mummy would have been placed in turn. Each would prepare the Pharaoh a little more for his journey to the Next World. Containers beneath one of the thrones contained melon seeds and almonds – food to see the Pharaoh through that journey.

• ADVENTURES IN THE REAL WORLD •

'Wonderful as this room was, it was only the antechamber, or entrance, to the Pharaoh's tomb. Carter carefully examined and removed the objects. Eventually all that was left were two statues guarding the door to another room, which Carter hoped was the burial chamber of Tutankhamun.

CAREFUL AS EVER

Carter was too much of a professional to rush into the exploration of the tomb. After all, he had spent 31 years in Egypt, so waiting a little longer wouldn't hurt, if it meant preserving his discovery. He oversaw the painstaking recording and removal of each object in the antechamber. A less patient person would have gone crazy wondering what treasures lay beyond the door at the end, but he maintained his methodical work rate. And because Carter had the loyalty of his team, no one sneaked in to get an early glimpse of the burial chamber.

• 1922 DISCOVERING THE TOMB OF TUTANKHAMUN •

'He wasn't disappointed. On 16th February 1923 that door was duly opened, and the full glory of the Pharaoh's burial chamber was revealed. Immediately in front of Carter was a carved golden wall. It turned out to be a shrine. Carter found the entrance to the shrine and inside was another, and another inside that!'

'Three shrines!' cried Sobek. 'That's amazing!'

'But that's not all. There was a fourth shrine, and inside that was a stone sarcophagus containing a nest of coffins, one inside the other. The innermost coffin, made of solid gold, contained Tutankhamun's mummy.

'Next to the nest of shrines was the heart of the tomb, which would have been emptied if tomb raiders had found it: the Treasury. And that name really does give a clue of the riches it contained. Just inside the door was a statue of the god Anubis, the god of mummies...'

• ADVENTURES IN THE REAL WORLD •

'Did you say "the god of mummies"?' asked Kututu. 'What a great idea to have a god of mummies.'

Mau smiled. 'Yes, and he's not just in charge of mummies. He's a god of the Afterlife, which is why it's good to have him in a tomb. But he's also a great help for those who are still living: Anubis is a patron of lost souls and the helpless.

'The statue guarding the Treasury was carved from wood and a wonderful work of art in itself. Anubis was depicted as a jackal, painted black all over except for bright gold trim around his eyes, ears and chest.'

Sobek interrupted: 'All right, you're the expert. Don't forget you were buried in this tomb as well. Just what was Anubis guarding, exactly?'

'You're right. I was in the tomb, but not in this special Treasury. So it gave me a thrill to read Howard Carter's words in the exhibition brochure yesterday. You can picture

• 1922 DISCOVERING THE TOMB OF TUTANKHAMUN •

yourself there with him when he first came across the Treasury and its wonders:

"Facing the doorway, on the farther side, stood the most beautiful monument that I have ever seen — so lovely that it made one gasp with wonder and admiration. The central portion of it consisted of a large shrine-shaped chest, completely overlaid with gold, and surmounted by a cornice of sacred cobras. Surrounding this, free-standing, were statues of the four tutelary goddesses of the dead — gracious figures with outstretched protective arms, so natural and lifelike in their pose, so pitiful and compassionate the expression on their faces, that one felt it almost sacrilege to look at them.'"

Sobek wanted to show off his knowledge to the others: 'That would be the canopic chest. Correct me if I'm wrong, Mau, but it would have held richly decorated vessels, each containing one of Tutankhamun's organs: his lungs, heart and stomach.'

• ADVENTURES IN THE REAL WORLD •

THE TREASURY

The Treasury, or sacred core of the tomb, contained Tutankhamun's most valuable possessions, and had somehow escaped looting for 3,000 years. When Carter and Carnarvon found this small room to the east of the Funerary Chamber, they both knew its importance. As Carter later wrote: 'a single glance sufficed to tell us that here, within this little chamber, lay the greatest treasures of the tomb.' The contents of the Treasury have provided the world with some of the best examples of Egyptian art and religious belief.

• 1922 DISCOVERING THE TOMB OF TUTANKHAMUN •

'You're right, Sobek. Those were packed because the Pharaoh would need them on his journey to the next world. The Treasury also contained games, tools and other objects that he would need, plus models of boats and barges to take him across the skies.

'And the Pharaoh wouldn't only need things for his journey to the Next World; he'd need servants to work for him.' Mau let that sentence sink in, as the other two imagined skeletons of royal servants buried with Tutankhamun. 'That's what the 413 carvings, called shabti statues, were for. The shabti performed the sort of tasks that workers and servants did on Earth — planting and harvesting, building and repairing — except they did it in the afterlife. In the autumn of 1925, three years after discovering the tomb, Carter finally opened the gold coffin that he knew contained Tutankhamun's mummy. There, covering the head and shoulders of the Boy King, was the gold mask, known as a funerary mask.

• ADVENTURES IN THE REAL WORLD •

THE FUNERARY MASK

Tutankhamun's 10 kg (22 lb) gold funerary mask is one of the most famous works of art in the world. For many people it's not just a beautiful likeness of a face but the immediate image of Egypt itself. The mask depicts the god Osiris, master of the Underworld and god of resurrection. On his shoulders, written in hieroglyphs, is a spell from the Book of the Dead. New research suggests that the mask might have been made for a queen because the name of Queen Neferneferuaten has been erased from the inside of the mask. More commonly known as Nefertiti, she was Tutankhamun's mother.

• 1922 DISCOVERING THE TOMB OF TUTANKHAMUN •

'The mask has become the most famous image of the entire tomb. It's huge and heavy, with the image of a god as its face. And guarding the statue, on its top, is a carving of the Royal Cobra Uraeus, representing the Protector Goddess, Wadjet.'

Mau looked serious. 'Howard Carter felt responsible for recording every bit of the tomb and all that it contained. Not just for himself, or even for future generations, but for another personal reason.'

'What could that have been?' asked Sobek.

'As a thank-you to his patron, Lord Carnarvon. In April 1923, just over four months after the discovery of Tutankhamun's tomb, Lord Carnarvon died in Cairo. He'd been bitten by a mosquito and cut the bite accidentally while shaving. The cut became infected and he died of blood poisoning. Some wild rumours said that a Pharaoh's curse was the cause of death, but Carter knew they were nonsense.

• ADVENTURES IN THE REAL WORLD •

'Loyal to the memory of his friend and patron, Howard Carter continued his work on the tomb with determination. It's thanks to their partnership that the world has come to know of the Boy King, and much more about our beloved Egypt.'

FRONT PAGE NEWS

By the time Howard Carter entered the main burial chamber of the tomb, the world was excited by the prospect. People were fascinated by the 'Boy King', who just months before was known only to a few Egyptian scholars. Reporters and photographers from around the world sped to Egypt, in order to cover this wonderful story. Most of them were to be disappointed, though. Carter had allowed only one reporter - H. V. Morton of London's Times newspaper - on to the site. The other reporters remained stuck in their hotels in Cairo. Morton's vivid descriptions of the site and its remarkable contents helped make Carter famous and turned Tutankhamun into Egypt's most famous pharaoh.

• 1922 DISCOVERING THE TOMB OF TUTANKHAMUN •

THE CURSE

Lord Carnarvon died of blood poisoning in Cairo on 5th April 1923, less than two months after the opening of Tutankhamun's tomb. Many members of the public, including Sherlock Holmes's creator Arthur Conan Doyle, believe that the lord died either because of a curse or because Tutankhamun's priests had spread a deadly substance on the tomb walls. Several others who had visited the tomb died within the next few years, although more than sixty tomb visitors (including Carter) lived much longer. But the idea of the curse remains popular. And it's true that a mummy's hand that Carter gave to his friend Bruce Ingham had a bracelet with the hieroglyph message: 'Cursed be he that moves my body. To him shall come fire, water and pestilence.' Within weeks, Ingham's house burned down and was later damaged by a flood.

· ADVENTURES IN THE REAL WORLD ·

EPILOGUE

The three animal mummies were silent, looking at all of the Tutankhamun treasures spread out among them.

Sobek looked up. 'Hmm. We "old timers" had never thought that these "modern folk" could live up to the memory of us ancient Egyptians. So Mau, did Howard Carter become famous around the world because of his discovery?'

'Yes and no. His photograph appeared in newspapers and magazines. And a new invention — cinema, with its moving images — showed him with some of the treasures. But news can become stale pretty quickly, and before long Carter faded from the pages of newspapers and cinema screens.

• ADVENTURES IN THE REAL WORLD •

'In 1932 Carter returned to London and spent his last years helping different museums build up and organise their Egyptian collections. He also toured the United States, giving lectures about Tutankhamun and Egypt.'

Kututu perked up. 'I don't think that Carter ever visited South America, but people there certainly knew about the Boy King. In Spanish he's known as "Rey Tut", or King Tut.'

'Yes, the world certainly knows the name of Tutankhamun, or Tut, even if fewer and fewer people can remember Howard Carter's name. Maybe he preferred it that way, but he certainly helped the world get to know that young Pharaoh.

'In fact, the world went a little crazy about Tutankhamun and Egypt. People began to dress or cut their hair a bit like ancient Egyptians. Jewellery and even buildings were made to look more "Egyptian". One of the hit songs of 1923 was "Old King Tut" and American President Herbert Hoover called his pet dog King Tut. The Three Stooges, a comedy team, even made

• 1922 DISCOVERING THE TOMB OF TUTANKHAMUN •

a short film called "We Want Our Mummy", all about King Rootin-Tootin.'

'Hmm. I don't like the idea of people making fun of our pharaohs,' sniffed Sobek.

Mau agreed. 'Carter might have opened the door for a lot of silliness, but he did oversee the most important archaeological discovery of the twentieth century. He'll be remembered for helping us all to learn more about King Tutankhamun and his times. This exhibition, and others like it touring the world over the years, have opened people's eyes about the wonders of ancient Egypt and its people.'

'And what about the local boy who discovered the tomb?' Sobek was a proud Egyptian, after all, and didn't like the idea of an outsider discovering Tutankhamun's tomb.

Mau smiled. 'You mean Hussein Abdel-Rassoul. He remained on the site, carrying out his duties. In 1925, Howard Carter took one of the heavy ornamental necklaces from the tomb, placed it carefully on Hussein and photographed him.

'Hussein cherished the photograph. He returned to the site every day, showing the photograph to tourists and letting them know that he had discovered the tomb in 1922. He continued for more than 70 years, and now his son carries on the tradition, letting the world know about his father's amazing discovery.'

TIMELINE

BC (some early dates, marked 'c.', are approximate)

c. 7000: The first settlements form along the Nile valley.

c. 3000: The kingdoms of Upper and Lower Egypt unite to form one kingdom.

c. 1353-1336: Reign of Tutankhamun's father, Pharaoh Akhenaten, who turns Egypt away from worshipping its traditional gods in favour of a single Sun God, Aten.

c. 1350: Birth of Ankhsenamun, daughter of Akhenaten and Nefertiti, and later wife of Tutankhamun.

c. 1345: Birth of Tutankhamun, named Tutankhaten at his birth.

c. 1336: Royal marriage of Tutankhamun and his half-sister Ankhsenamun.

c. 1336: Death of Akhenaten. Tutankhamun becomes Pharaoh, with Ankhsenamun as his Queen. Ay serves as vizier to the young Pharaoh.

• ADVENTURES IN THE REAL WORLD •

c. 1336: The Pharaoh, with Ay's advice, returns Egypt to the old religion and its worship of many gods. His name is changed to Tutankhamun to reflect this change. Many monuments from Akhenaten's reign are destroyed.

c. 1334: Egypt's capital is returned to Thebes, where shrines to the god Amun are built.

1323: Tutankhamun dies. Ay succeeds him as Pharaoh.

332: Alexander the Great conquers Egypt and founds Alexandria. A Macedonian (Greek-culture) dynasty begins.

30: Queen Cleopatra commits suicide after her troops are defeated by the Romans. Egypt comes under Roman rule.

AD

642: Arab conquest of Egypt.

1517: Egypt absorbed into the Ottoman Empire.

1798-1801: Napoleon Bonaparte's troops invade but are defeated by British and Turkish troops. French and British involvement sparks interest in Egypt among Europeans.

1805: Ottoman leader Muhammad Ali establishes a dynasty that will govern Egypt for nearly 150 years.

• 1922 DISCOVERING THE TOMB OF TUTANKHAMUN •

1874: Howard Carter, the youngest of eleven children, is born in Kensington, London.

1891: William Amherst arranges an interview for Howard Carter with Percy Newberry, who had been working at Beni Hasan, Egypt. Carter is soon hired as a trainee tracer.

1892: Carter is appointed Principal Artist to the Egyptian Exploration Fund for the excavations at Deir el-Bahari, the burial place of Queen Hatshepsut. He works with the famous Egyptologist, Flinders Petrie.

1893: Howard Carter joins Professor Édouard Naville and spends six years drawing in the temple at Deir el-Bahari.

1899: Gaston Maspero, Director-General of the Department of Egyptian Antiquities, hires Carter as Inspector General of Monuments for Upper Egypt.

1905: Carter resigns as Inspector General after a violent dispute between his men and some French tourists at the Saqqara Pyramid, one of the monuments under Carter's care.

1905-1907: Carter has no fixed job but works at various sites, including the Valley of the Kings with Theodore M. Davis of the United States.

• ADVENTURES IN THE REAL WORLD •

1907-1914: Maspero introduces Carter to Lord Carnarvon, a wealthy amateur Egyptologist. Carnarvon supports Carter on digs near Thebes and in northern Egypt.

1914: Davis gives up his concession to dig in the Valley of the Kings and Carnarvon takes it over. Plans by Carter and Carnarvon to dig there are suspended by the start of the First World War.

1917: Carter convinces Carnarvon to pay for excavations in the Valley of the Kings in search of Tutankhamun's tomb. For five years the digs reveal no trace of the tomb.

1922: Carnarvon tires of spending money on unsuccessful digs, but agrees to pay for one more dig in search of the pharaoh Tutankhamun's tomb.

4th November: Twelve-year-old Hussein Abdel-Rassoul uncovers what turns out to be a step leading to Tutankhamun's tomb.

5th November: Carter sends a telegram to Carnarvon, telling him of the exciting discovery, but covers the stairs again until Carnarvon's arrival.

26th November: Carter, watched by Carnarvon and his daughter Lady Evelyn Herbert, opens a gap in the tomb door and observes 'wonderful things' inside.

• 1922 DISCOVERING THE TOMB OF TUTANKHAMUN •

27th November: Carter, Carnarvon and Lady Evelyn Herbert explore the tomb's antechamber and annexe (next to it), noticing another sealed door leading to another chamber.

December: News of the discovery reaches the wider world and creates a sensation. Reporters and photographers rush to Egypt, interrupting Carter's work.

1923:

9th January: Carnarvon signs a deal with *The Times* of London, allowing only that newspaper permission to visit the site and report.

16th February: Carter opens the sealed doorway from the antechamber into the burial chamber.

1923-1932: Carter is in charge of recording the exact contents of the tomb. He also writes and publishes an account of its discovery and goes on lecture tours in Europe and the United States.

1932: Carter completes his work at the tomb and returns to England.

1939: Howard Carter dies in London on 2nd March.

• ADVENTURES IN THE REAL WORLD •

GLOSSARY

Afterlife: According to ancient Egyptian religious beliefs, a place that a dead person's spirit enters for eternity.

Alexandria: A port in northern Egypt, where the River Nile flows into the Mediterranean Sea.

antiquities: Ancient objects, monuments and buildings that are valuable and need protection.

archaeologist: A person who uncovers evidence of how people lived long ago.

aristocrat: A person with high social standing, and often great wealth, because of the family that they were born into.

British Museum: One of the world's great museums, located in central London and containing many objects from around the world, including a vast Egyptian collection.

Cairo: The capital of modern Egypt, founded in AD 969 and now the largest city in Africa.

coffin: A box, sometimes richly decorated, in which a dead person is buried or laid in a tomb.

concession: Legal permission to carry out work in a particular place.

• 1922 DISCOVERING THE TOMB OF TUTANKHAMUN •

cornice: A horizontal strip of decoration or carving running along the top of a structure.

courier: Someone responsible for delivering messages, often relating to officials.

dynasty: A period of rule in a country during which rulers were all from the same family.

Egyptologist: An archaeologist whose special interest is in Ancient Egypt.

empire: A groups of nations or large area ruled by one government; an empire is often the result of military conquest.

excavate: To dig in an organised manner, either to prepare to build or to reveal something that has been buried.

exhibition: A temporary display of items not usually seen in a museum, often on loan from another museum.

exotic: From a far-off land.

expedition: A journey taken by a group of people with a particular goal in mind.

First World War: A war, beginning in Europe in 1914 but involving many countries from other regions by the time it ended in 1918.

• ADVENTURES IN THE REAL WORLD •

heka: The ancient Egyptian word for magic and also the name (Heka) of the Egyptian god of medicine.

herbal: Relating to plants that are used in medicine.

hieroglyphics: A form of writing, as in ancient Egypt, that uses pictures or symbols to stand for words.

jackal: A wolf-like animal native to most parts of Africa.

ma'at: The ancient Egyptian term used to describe harmony and balance.

malaria: A serious, and sometimes deadly, disease that is carried by mosquitoes.

mummified: Specially prepared and dried, then wrapped to remain preserved. People and animals became mummies in ancient Egypt.

Napoleon Bonaparte: A powerful French military leader who invaded Egypt in 1798, before being driven off by the British army.

noble: Describing someone from a privileged social group, based on their background.

Ottoman Empire: An empire, based in what is now Istanbul, Turkey, that controlled much of southeastern Europe, Western Asia and North Africa from the 1300s to the early 1900s.

patron: Someone who provides support (and usually money) to another person, organisation or cause.

pharaoh: The king, or supreme ruler, in ancient Egypt.

portrait: A painting, drawing or sculpture of a person or an animal.

procession: A slow progression of people or vehicles during a ceremony.

Pyramids: In Egypt, the term usually refers to the group of huge pyramids built in Giza, near modern-day Cairo. The Pyramids housed the remains of early Pharaohs.

rubble: Worthless stone and other small rocks.

sacrilege: Deliberate damage to or disrespect of something that is considered holy.

sarcophagus: A stone coffin.

shrine: A sacred place that is devoted to something worshipped, like a god.

Sphinx: A huge ancient statue near the Pyramids of Giza, with the head of a human and the body of a lion.

spoil: Earth and rock dug up at an excavation.

• ADVENTURES IN THE REAL WORLD •

telegram: An early form of message sent electrically along wires over long distances.

transparent: Clear, so that objects can be seen through it.

trinket: A small, and not very expensive ornament.

tutelary: Acting as a guardian or protector.

Upper Egypt: The southern part of Egypt, that is upstream (further south) along the River Nile.

vizier: The highest ranking government official in ancient Egypt, appointed by the Pharaoh and acting as his adviser.

INDEX

A
Abdel Rassoul, Hussein 90, 116, 120
Afterlife 10, 22, 69–70, 104, 107, 122
Akhenaten 38–39, 60–61, 72–73, 117–118
Amherst, Lord 20–21, 24–25, 30–31, 41, 119
Amun 61, 118
Anubis 103–104

B
Bonaparte, Napoleon 17, 32, 118, 124
burial chamber 102–103, 110, 121

C
Carnarvon, Lord 54–55, 75–81, 83–89, 93–95, 97–99, 100, 106, 109, 111, 120-121
Carter, Howard 11, 14–20, 24, 30, 33–39, 41–50, 52–54, 55, 75–92, 94–95, 97–100, 102–104, 106–107, 109–111, 113–115, 119-121
Conan Doyle, Sir Arthur 111

D
Davis, Theodore M. 46 79–80, 119
Didlington Hall 20–21, 31

F
Flinders Petrie, Sir William Matthew 37–39, 42–43, 47, 119
Funerary Chamber 106
funerary mask 107–109

G
gold 9, 11, 50, 66, 103–105, 107–108

H
heka 71, 124
Highclere Castle 85

Hoover, Herbert 114

L
London 14–16, 18, 21, 110, 114, 119, 121–122

M
ma'at 71, 124
Maspero, Gaston 42–43, 119–120
Memphis 53
mummies, mummification 8, 10–11, 20, 30, 58–59, 70, 103–104, 113, 124

N
Nefertiti 108, 117
Newberry, Percy 30–31, 33–34, 37, 41, 47, 119
Nile 28, 33, 44, 48, 62, 65, 69, 79, 117, 122, 126

O
Osiris 22, 108
Ottoman Empire 32, 81, 118, 124

P
Pharaoh's curse 109, 111

Pyramids 21, 29, 51, 60, 76, 119, 125

R
Rameses VI 90
Rosetta Stone 25

S
Saqqara 49, 53, 119
Sphinx 21, 60, 125

T
Thebes 48, 65, 72, 78, 118, 120
tomb robbers 50, 73, 100
Tutankhamun 4, 7, 9–10, 14, 29, 33, 36, 46–47, 49–50, 54, 57–65, 70–73, 80–81, 83, 87, 89–90, 97–99, 102–103, 105–111, 113–115, 117–118, 120

V
Valley of the Kings 5, 46–49, 54, 65, 79–80, 82, 84–85, 87, 90, 119–120
Vizier 63, 72, 117, 126

W
Wadjet 109